Contents

Chapter **1**
Getting started

Note to teachers: MSW Logo is freely available as a download from www.softronix.com. The exercises in this text use standard LOGO commands which will work in other commercial versions of the language. Some differences are likely to occur when editing, saving and loading procedures or using colour.

The worksheets referred to throughout the text can be downloaded as MS Word 2000 files from the resources section at www.payne-gallway.co.uk/logo

Before pupils can complete Chapter 1 the files **maze.bmp** and **maze2.bmp** must be placed in the MSW Logo directory located at **c:\MSWLogo**. If you have not installed MSW Logo in this location pupils will need to be given additional instructions when they are asked to load the maze bitmaps on pages 9 and 11. These files can be downloaded from the resources section at www.payne-gallway.co.uk/logo.

Getting started with LOGO

In this chapter you will start to learn about LOGO. This is a computer programming language that will teach you about computer control by writing programs to move a small shape called a turtle around the drawing screen.

Note:

Make sure your teacher has given you a copy of **Worksheet 1**.

Loading LOGO

 Load **MSW Logo**. You can do this in one of two ways.

 Either double-click the **MSW Logo** icon.

Or click **Start** at the bottom left of the screen, then click **Programs**, then click

 Click **OK** if any message boxes appear.

Your screen will look like Figure 1.1.

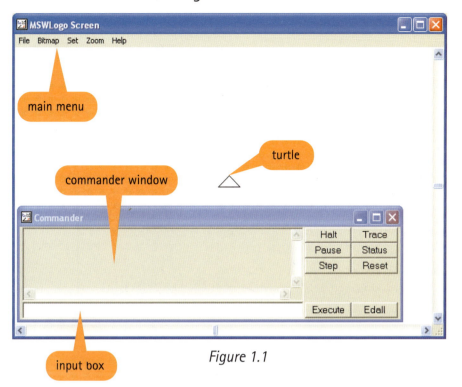

Figure 1.1

The turtle is the triangle in the middle of the drawing screen. The turtle's head shows you the direction it is facing. As the turtle moves it draws a line with its pen. You tell the turtle how to move by giving it commands. The turtle always moves in the direction that its head is pointing.

Figure 1.2

Making the turtle move

The simplest way to make the turtle move is by entering commands one at a time in the input box. The simplest commands in LOGO are; forward, back, right and left. Instead of entering these words you can use the shorter versions fd, bk, rt and lt, which mean exactly the same thing. We'll try these commands out now.

Note:

LOGO was first used to move a small robot connected to the computer around the floor. These robots were plastic domes on wheels. They looked a lot like a turtle. That's why we call the triangle shape on the screen a turtle.

fd

To move the turtle forward you must enter this command followed by the number of steps you want it to move.

Let's try using this command to move the turtle 100 steps forward.

Tip:

Always put a space after an **fd** command before entering the number of steps you want the turtle to move forward.

▶ Click in the input box.

▶ Type fd 100

▶ Press Enter.
The turtle will move 100 steps forward.

Figure 1.3

rt

To turn the turtle right you must enter this command followed by a number for the angle you want its head to turn through.
The angle is measured in degrees.

Let's try using this command to turn the turtle to the right through an angle of 90 degrees.

▶ Click in the input box.

▶ Type rt 90

▶ Press Enter.
The turtle will turn to the right through an angle of 90 degrees.

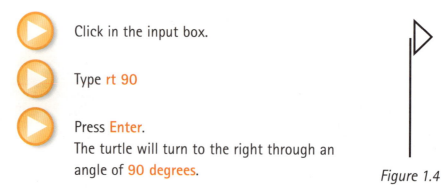
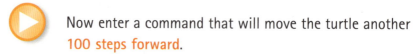

Figure 1.4

▶ Now enter a command that will move the turtle another 100 steps forward.

lt

To turn the turtle left you must enter this command followed by a number for the angle you want its head to turn through.

Let's try using this command to turn the turtle to the left through an angle of 90 degrees.

Click in the input box.

 Type **lt 90**

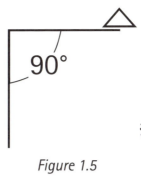

90°

 Press **Enter**.
The turtle will turn to the left through an angle of **90 degrees**.

Figure 1.5

 Now enter a command that will move the turtle another **100 steps forward**.

Have you drawn a line like the one below?

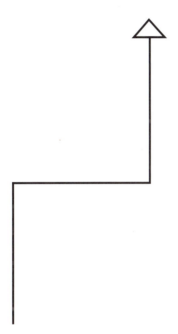

Figure 1.6

Before we carry on and draw anything else we'll learn how to wipe the drawing screen clean with the **clearscreen** command.

clearscreen

This command clears the drawing screen and wipes away everything the turtle has drawn. The shorter version of this command is **cs** – this is the one we'll use.

 Click in the input box.

 Type **cs** and press **Enter**.
The drawing screen will be wiped clean.

Tip:

Always press **Enter** after typing a command in the input window - nothing will happen until you do!

Tip:

A message saying, **'I don't know how to...'** means there was either a spelling mistake or space missing in the last command you entered.

5

Now we can draw something else!

back

So far we've learned how to move the turtle forward and make it turn left or right. The turtle can also move back. The command we use for this is back. The shorter version of this command is bk – this is the one we'll use. To move the turtle back you must enter this command followed by the number of steps back you want it to move.

 Click in the input box.

 Type cs and press Enter to clear the drawing screen.

 Enter these commands:
fd 100
rt 90
fd 50

Let's try using the back command to move the turtle 100 steps back.

 Type bk 100

 Press Enter.
The turtle will move 100 steps back.

You should have drawn a letter T like the one shown below.

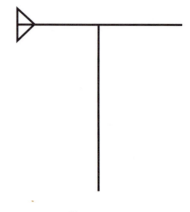

Figure 1.7

Tip:

Remember to press **Enter** after typing each command in the input window.

hideturtle

To see this letter without the turtle in the way, we need to use another new command, hideturtle – or ht for short.

 Click in the input box.

 Type ht and press Enter to hide the turtle.

The turtle will disappear. Your letter T should now look like the one shown in Figure 1.8.

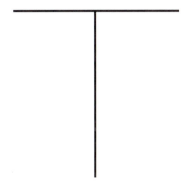

Figure 1.8

Tip:
The **hideturtle** command is useful when you've drawn a shape or pattern and you want to see it without having the turtle in the way. Always remember to use the **showturtle** command when you've finished!

showturtle

To get the turtle to come back we must use the showturtle command – or st for short.

 Click in the input box.

 Type st and press Enter to make the turtle come back.

The turtle will reappear and your letter T should now look like the one shown in Figure 1.7.

home

This command moves the turtle to the centre of the screen. There isn't a shorter version of this command so we need to type in the whole word to use it. Let's try using this command.

 Click in the input box.

 Type cs and press Enter to clear the drawing screen.

Enter these commands to move the turtle away from the centre of the screen:

fd 100

rt 45

fd 100

The turtle will move away from the centre of the screen and draw a line like the one shown below.

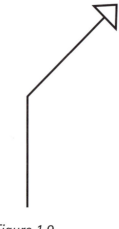

Figure 1.9

 Type home and press Enter.

The turtle will move back to the centre of the screen drawing a line as it moves. You should now have a shape like the one shown below on the screen.

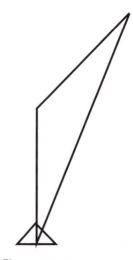

Figure 1.10

Tip:

Moving the turtle back to the centre of the screen with the **home** command can be a useful way to finish off a shape or drawing.

Now for something amazing!

So far you have used the basic LOGO commands fd, rt, lt and bk to make the turtle move around the screen. You are going to practise using these commands a little bit more now. Follow the steps below to get started.

 Click Bitmap and Load on the main menu at the top of the screen.

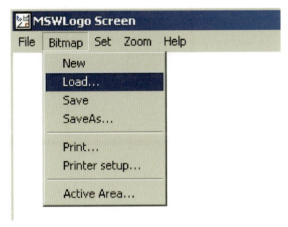

Figure 1.11

The file we need to load is called Maze.

 Click on the file called Maze and click Open.

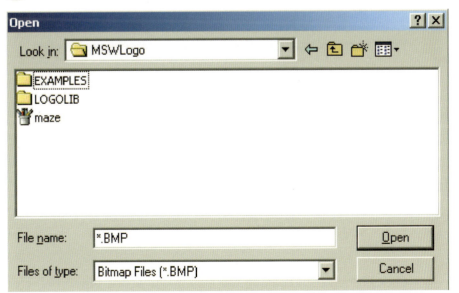

Figure 1.12

Note:

Your teacher will tell you where to find the **Maze** file if you can't see it in the list of files on your screen.

You will see the maze shown below displayed on the drawing screen.

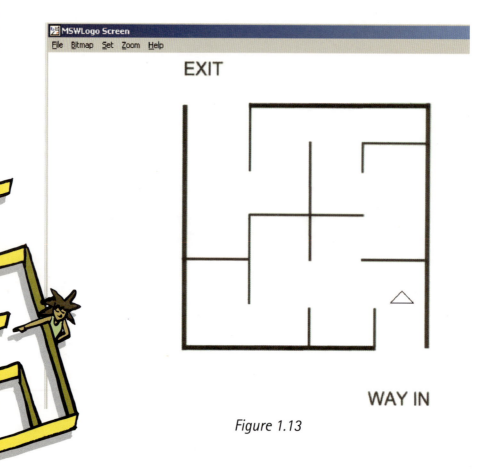

Figure 1.13

Use the LOGO commands that you have learned for forward, back, left and right to guide the turtle through the maze without touching any of the walls.

Write each command on Worksheet 1 in the column labelled 1st attempt.

Next see if you can improve on your first attempt and get the turtle out of the maze using fewer commands. To get started we need to clear the drawing screen and load the maze file again – follow the steps below to do this.

Type CS and press Enter to clear the drawing screen.

Click Bitmap then Load on the main menu at the top of the screen.

Click on the file called Maze and then click OK.

 Now guide the turtle through the maze again but with fewer commands. Write each command you use on Worksheet 1 in the column labelled 2nd attempt.

How many commands did you use the second time? Was it fewer than the first time? Compare the commands on your worksheet with someone else in your class – how did they do and was anything different about their commands?

Time for another maze?

If you have time, follow the instructions below to load another maze that you can guide the turtle through.

 Click Bitmap and Load on the main menu at the top of the screen.

The file we need to load this time is called Maze2.

 Click on the file called Maze2 and click OK.

You will see the maze shown below displayed on the drawing screen.

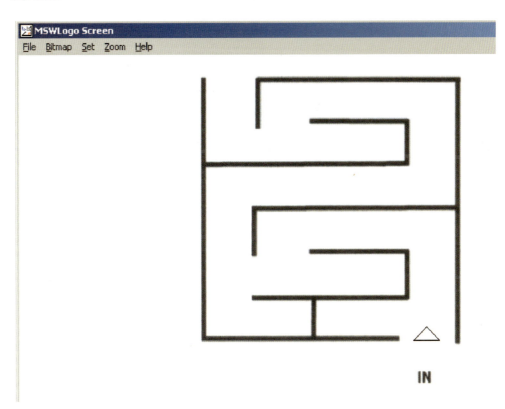

Figure 1.14

Guide the turtle through this maze without touching any of the walls.

That's almost everything you need to know about LOGO basics. The last command we'll learn about in this chapter is bye – this is described below.

bye

This command is used to leave MSW Logo. There isn't a shorter version of this command so we need to type in the whole word to use it.

 Click in the input box.

 Type bye

 Press Enter and LOGO will close down.

Chapter 2
More LOGO commands

In this chapter you will learn to use more LOGO commands.

Before we get started make sure your teacher has given you a copy of Worksheet 2.1.

 Load MSW Logo.

Now we can carry on, learn some more commands and use the turtle to draw some more.

 What do you think these commands will draw?
Sketch your answer on Worksheet 2.1 in the first box labelled
What I think the turtle will draw.

rt 45
fd 100
rt 90
fd 100
lt 90
fd 100
rt 90
fd 100
lt 90
fd 100
ht

 Click in the input box.

 Enter the commands shown above.

Note:

Worksheet 2.1 can be downloaded from the resources section at www.payne-gallway.co.uk/logo

Tip:
Remember to put a space between each command and the number of steps or angle and press **Enter** after each one!

Tip:

Use the **cs** command to clear the drawing screen - look back to **page 5** if you can't remember how to do this.

 Were you right? Sketch what the turtle did draw on Worksheet 2.1 in the first box labelled What the turtle did draw.

 Clear the drawing screen.

 What do you think these commands will draw?
Sketch your answer on **Worksheet 2.1** in the second box labelled What I think the turtle will draw.

st
fd 100
rt 90
fd 50
rt 90
fd 50
rt 90
fd 100
lt 90
fd 50
lt 90
fd 50
ht

 Click in the input box.

 Enter the commands shown above.

 Were you right? Sketch what the turtle did draw on Worksheet 2.1 in the first box labelled What the turtle did draw.

Next we'll learn how to move the turtle around without leaving lines behind on the drawing screen. We will use the penup command to do this.

penup

This command lifts the pen up. This stops the turtle from drawing as it moves. The shorter version of this command is pu – this is the one we'll use.

 Click in the input box.

Type **pu** and press **Enter**.

Enter these commands:
rt 90
fd 50

These commands will turn the turtle right 90 degrees and move it forward 50 steps without drawing a line.

It is important to remember to put the pen down again before you try making the turtle move and draw again. The **pendown** command is used to do this.

pendown

This command puts the pen back down after it has been lifted up to make the turtle start drawing again as it moves along. The shorter version of this command is **pd** – this is the one we'll use.

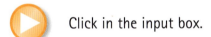 Click in the input box.

Type **pd** and press **Enter**.

 Enter these commands:
lt 90
fd 50

These commands will turn the turtle left 90 degrees and move it forward 50 steps drawing a line as it moves.

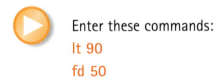 Enter these commands:
lt 90
fd 50

Note:

Worksheet 2.2 can be downloaded from the resources section at www.payne-gallway.co.uk/logo

Have you drawn a letter 'h' like the one shown below?

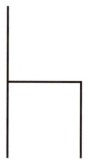

Figure 2.1

Now try this

Before we get started make sure your teacher has given you a copy of Worksheet 2.2.

The LOGO commands we've used so far are: forward, left, right, back, penup and pendown. In the last example we used these commands to draw a letter 'h'.

 You are going to try and draw your initials using these commands. Here are the initials ht – Harry Turtle?

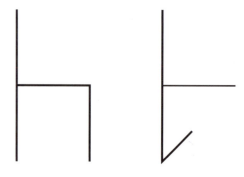

Figure 2.2

Tip:

Use the **ht** command to hide the turtle and the **st** command to show the turtle. Look back to **page 7** if you can't remember how to do this.

 Use the LOGO commands that you have learned so far for forward, left, right, back, penup and pendown to draw your own initials.

 Write each command on Worksheet 2.2 in the column labelled 1st attempt.

 Hide the turtle when you've finished.

Next see if you can improve on your first attempt and get the turtle to draw the letters for your initials using fewer commands.

 To get started you will need to clear the drawing screen and make sure you can see the turtle.

 Write each command on Worksheet 2.2 in the column labelled 2nd attempt.

When you've finished print out your initials – follow the instructions below to do this.

 Click Bitmap and Print on the main menu at the top of the screen.

Figure 2.3

 Choose the printer you want to use and click OK. Ask your teacher if you're not sure which printer to choose.

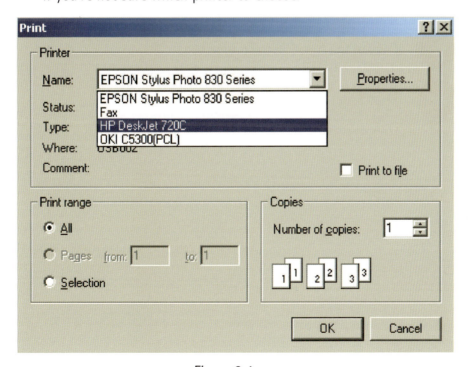

Figure 2.4

Note:

It doesn't matter if you don't get this exactly right the first or second time - just clear the drawing screen and try again! Each time you have another go write the commands you used in the next empty column on **Worksheet 2.2**.

Some other things to try

Use the LOGO commands forward, left, right, back, penup and pendown to make the turtle draw some of the drawings below.

Tip:

Use the **cs** command to clear the screen before starting on a new drawing.

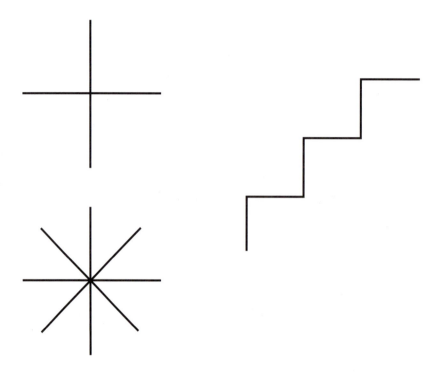

Figure 2.5

That's all you need to learn about basic LOGO commands. In the next chapter you will learn how to use these commands to draw simple shapes like squares and triangles.

 Click in the input box and type bye.

 Press Enter to close LOGO down.

Chapter **3**
Drawing simple shapes

In the last two chapters you learned how to use simple LOGO commands to make the turtle move around the drawing screen. In this chapter you will learn how to use the same commands to draw simple shapes.

Before we get started on this part of the chapter make sure your teacher has given you a copy of Worksheet 3.1.

 Load MSW Logo.

Note:
Worksheet 3.1 can be downloaded from the resources section at www.payne-gallway.co.uk/logo

Drawing simple shapes

 What shape do you think the commands shown below will draw? Sketch your answer on Worksheet 3.1 in the first box labelled What I think the turtle will draw.

fd 50
rt 90
fd 50
rt 90
fd 50
rt 90
fd 50

Tip:
Try using a piece of squared paper to help. Imagine you are the turtle and each square is worth ten steps forward. What would these commands make you draw?

 Click in the input box and enter the commands shown above.

 Were you right? Sketch what the turtle did draw on Worksheet 3.1 in the first box labelled What the turtle did draw.

Let's draw another shape like this one.

What do you think these commands will draw?
Will it look much different from the last shape?
Sketch your answer on Worksheet 3.1 in the second box labelled
What I think the turtle will draw.

fd 200

rt 90

fd 200

rt 90

fd 200

rt 90

fd 200

Click in the input box and clear the drawing screen.

Enter the commands shown above.

Were you right? Sketch what the turtle did draw on Worksheet 3.1 in the second box labelled What the turtle did draw.

Think about the differences between the commands you entered to draw this shape compared with the first shape. What is it about these commands that made the second shape look different?
Write your answer on Worksheet 3.1 in the second box labelled Why is this shape different?

Now we'll draw a different shape.

Click in the input box and clear the drawing screen.

Enter the commands shown below.
fd 200

lt 120

fd 200

lt 120

fd 200

lt 120

Question:

Which commands are different this time? Think about the commands that are still the same. Will some commands always have to be the same to make the turtle draw this sort of shape?

Did the turtle draw a triangle like the one shown below?

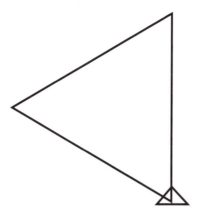

Figure 3.1

Now you're going to draw two more triangles.

 Work out a list of commands that will draw a triangle BIGGER than the first one.

 Write your commands on Worksheet 3.1 in the third box labelled Commands needed to draw a BIGGER triangle.

 Click in the input box and enter your list of commands. Were you right – did your commands draw a bigger triangle?

 Now work out a list of commands that will draw a triangle SMALLER than the first one.

 Write your commands on Worksheet 3.1 in the last box labelled Commands needed to draw a SMALLER triangle.

 Click in the input box and enter your list of commands. Were you right – did your commands draw a smaller triangle?

You should have a set of three triangles on the screen that look something like the ones shown below.

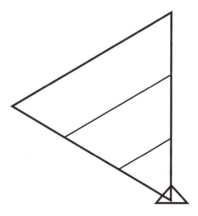

Figure 3.2

Question:

Which commands will need to be different this time? Think about the squares that you have just drawn. Which commands will always have to be the same to make the turtle draw a triangle?

Some other things to try

Before we get started on this part of the chapter make sure your teacher has given you a copy of Worksheet 3.2.

 Clear the drawing screen.

 Work out a list of commands that will draw a shape like the one shown below.

Figure 3.3

 Write your commands on Worksheet 3.2 in the first box labelled Commands needed to draw this shape.

 Enter your list of commands.

 Work out a list of commands that will draw a shape like the one shown in Figure 3.4.

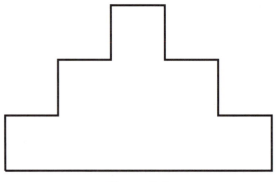

Figure 3.4

Tip:

Use the **cs** command to clear the drawing screen - look back to page 5 if you can't remember how to do this.

Write your commands down on Worksheet 3.2 in the second box labelled Commands needed to draw this shape.

 Clear the drawing screen and enter your list of commands.

Work out a list of commands that will draw a shape like the one shown in Figure 3.5.

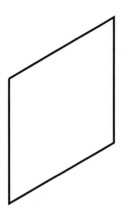

Figure 3.5

 Write your commands on Worksheet 3.2 in the last box labelled Commands needed to draw this shape.

 Clear the drawing screen and enter your list of commands.

That's all you need to learn about using basic LOGO commands to draw simple shapes. In the next chapter you will learn how to draw these and other shapes more efficiently using the repeat command.

 Click in the input box.

 Type bye and press Enter to close LOGO down.

Chapter 4
Repeating commands

Note:

Worksheet 4.1 can be downloaded from the resources section at www.payne-gallway.co.uk/logo

In the last chapter you used basic LOGO commands to draw simple shapes like squares and triangles. In this chapter you will learn about the repeat command and how it can be used to draw these and other shapes more efficiently.

Before we get started on this part of the chapter make sure your teacher has given you a copy of Worksheet 4.1.

 Load MSW Logo.

The repeat command

When you drew a square at the beginning of the last chapter the same commands had to be entered four times to draw the four sides of the shape. LOGO can do this much more efficiently using the repeat command. There isn't a shorter version of this command so we'll need to type in the whole word to use it.

Let's try drawing a square using the repeat command.

 Click in the input box and clear the drawing screen.

 Enter this command:

repeat 4[fd 50 rt 90]

This command has repeated the commands inside the square brackets four times to draw the square. Using a repeat command to draw this shape is much more efficient because fewer commands are needed to do exactly the same thing.

Tip:

Take care to put a space before the square brackets and in between the commands inside the square brackets.

24

Let's try drawing a triangle using the repeat command.

 Click in the input box and clear the drawing screen.

 Enter this command:
repeat 3[fd 200 rt 120]
This command has repeated the commands inside the square brackets three times to draw the triangle.

Polygons

The square we've just drawn is an example of a regular polygon. These are shapes with sides that are all the same length separated by equal angles.

A square has *four sides* and *four equal angles* of 90 degrees inside it that add up to 360 degrees. To draw a square with sides 100 steps long we used a repeat command to move 100 steps forward and turn right 90 degrees four times.

The repeat command we used was repeat 4[fd 50 rt 90]

Now we're going to use the repeat command to draw some more regular polygons.

 Look at the commands shown below.
How many sides do you think each shape will have?
Write your answers on Worksheet 4.1 next to each command in the column labelled How many sides?

Repeat 5 [fd 200 rt 72]

Repeat 6 [fd 150 lt 60]

Repeat 8 [fd 175 lt 45]

Tip:
Being able to write efficient instructions by using commands like **repeat** is a good way to show that your ICT skills are getting better.

Tip:
The sides of a regular polygon are always the same length. The angles inside a regular polygon are always equal and add up to 360 degrees.

What will each shape look like?
Sketch your answer on Worksheet 4.1 next to each command in the column labelled "What this shape will look like"

Now try entering each one of these repeat commands.

Were you right about the number of sides each shape would have?
Were you right about how each shape would look?
Sketch what the turtle drew when you entered each repeat command in the column labelled What the turtle drew on Worksheet 4.1

More polygons

Note:

Worksheet 4.2 can be downloaded from the resources section at www.payne-gallway.co.uk/logo

Before we get started on this part of the chapter make sure your teacher has given you a copy of Worksheet 4.2.

Work out the repeat commands needed to make the turtle draw the shapes shown below. You can give each shape whatever length of side you want to.

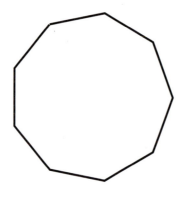

Figure 4.1

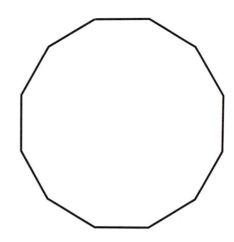

Figure 4.2

Hint:

Count the number of sides on each shape. If you divide 360 by the number of sides this will give you the angle you need to use inside your repeat command.

Write each repeat command next to its picture on Worksheet 4.2 in the box labelled Repeat command needed to draw this shape.

Enter the repeat commands you have written on Worksheet 4.2.

Something else to try

The drawing below is one that you might have worked out a list of commands for at the end of chapter 2. Can you work out a repeat command that will make the turtle draw this?

Tip:

You drew something similar in **Chapter 1**. Try looking back at the commands for this on **page 5**.

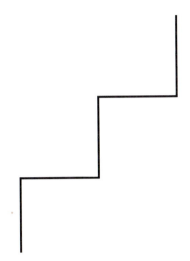

Figure 4.3

The drawing below is another one you might have worked out a list of commands for at the end of Chapter 2. Can you work out a repeat command that make the turtle draw this?

Tip:

Your teacher will give you a list of these commands if you don't have them. Look at the commands. Which commands are repeated? How many times are these commands repeated?

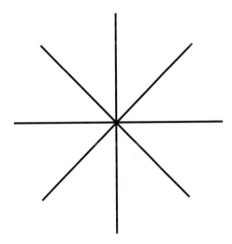

Figure 4.4

Tip:

Don't worry if you can't get this right first time, just use the **cs** command to clear the screen before trying again!

Tip:

If you can't remember how to close LOGO down look back at the instructions on page 12.

 Use the right and forward commands inside a repeat command to make the turtle draw the pattern shown below.

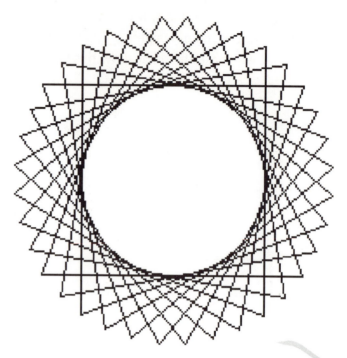

Figure 4.5

That's almost everything you need to know about drawing simple shapes and polygons using the repeat command.

 Close LOGO down.

Chapter 5
Procedures

In the last chapter you learned how to use the repeat command to draw shapes like squares, triangles and circles. In this chapter you will learn how to draw these and other shapes by creating procedures.

Before we get started on this part of the chapter make sure your teacher has given you a copy of Worksheet 5.1.

 Load MSW Logo.

Creating procedures

To draw a shape without typing the same commands over and over again you must create a procedure.
A procedure is a small computer program that does one simple thing – like drawing a square. To do this the commands that draw the shape must be entered and given a name. This set of commands is then called a procedure. Once this has been done LOGO will draw the shape when you enter the name of the procedure.

Let's try doing this by creating a procedure to draw a square.

 From the main menu select File, Edit...

Figure 5.1

Note:

Worksheet 5.1 can be downloaded from the resources section at www.payne-gallway.co.uk/logo

You will see a dialogue box like the one shown below.

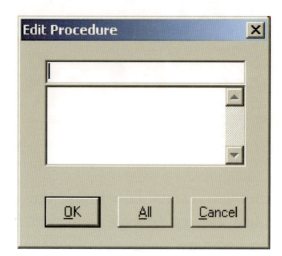

Figure 5.2

 Type square

 Click OK. The Editor dialogue box will appear – it should look like the one shown below.

Figure 5.3

to is the LOGO command to define the start of the procedure.
Square is the name we have given to this procedure.
end is the LOGO command that finishes this procedure.

To create this procedure we need to put the commands that draw the square in between the to and end commands. Follow the steps below to do this.

 Click after the word square on the first line.

 Press Enter.

 Type repeat 4[fd 100 rt 90]

This is the same repeat command we used to draw a square in the last chapter. Your procedure should look like the one shown below.

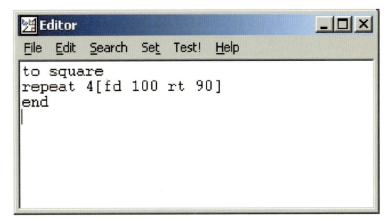

Figure 5.4

 Click File, Save and Exit on the Editor dialogue box menu.

Figure 5.5

All you need to do now to make LOGO draw the square is enter the name of this procedure – let's try this.

 Click in the input box.

 Type square

 Press Enter.
LOGO will run the procedure and the turtle will draw a square.

Next we'll try creating a procedure that will draw a triangle using a repeat command.

 Click in the input box.

 Type edit "triangle and press Enter.
The Editor dialogue box will appear – this is another way to create a procedure without using the main menu.

Figure 5.6

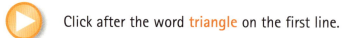 Click after the word triangle on the first line.

 Press Enter.

 Type repeat 3[fd 200 rt 120]

This is the same repeat command we used to draw a triangle in the last chapter. Your procedure should look like the one shown below.

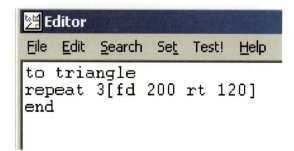

Figure 5.7

 Click File, Save and Exit on the Editor dialogue box menu.

Figure 5.8

All you need to do now to make LOGO draw the triangle is enter the name of this procedure – let's try this.

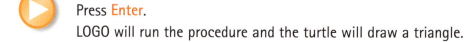 Click in the input box.

Type triangle

Press Enter.
LOGO will run the procedure and the turtle will draw a triangle.

Now try this

You should have the commands that will draw the shape below written down on Worksheet 3.2.

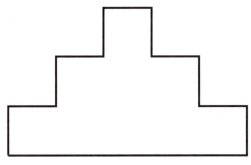

Figure 5.9

 Look at these commands and decide which ones you can replace with a repeat command – try out your new repeat command.

 Create a procedure called blocks that uses this repeat command to draw the shape.

Patterns and procedures

Procedures can be combined with other LOGO commands such as repeat. We'll try doing this to draw a pattern using the square procedure inside a repeat command.

 Click in the input box.

 Type cs and press Enter to clear the drawing screen.

 Type repeat 2[square rt 60]

 Press Enter.
The turtle will draw two squares like those shown below.

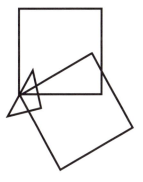

Figure 5.10

Note:

If you don't have the commands to draw this shape written down ask your teacher for them.

If we repeat this command more times the turtle will start to build up a pattern with the square shape – let's try this.

▶ Click in the input box.

▶ Type **cs** and press **Enter** to clear the drawing screen.

▶ Type **repeat 6[square rt 60]**

▶ Press **Enter**.
The turtle will draw the pattern shown below.

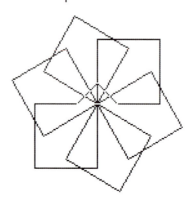

Figure 5.11

What do you think the pattern will look like if the commands inside the square bracket are repeated ten times? Let's try this and see what happens!

▶ Click in the input box.

▶ Type **cs** and press **Enter** to clear the drawing screen.

▶ Type **repeat 10[square rt 60]**

▶ Press **Enter**.
The turtle will draw the pattern shown below.

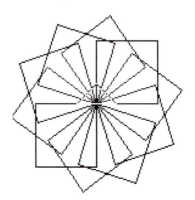

Figure 5.12

This pattern looks like a flower but there's something missing – the stalk. What LOGO command do you think will make the turtle add a stalk to the flower so that it looks like the one shown below?

 Work out a LOGO command that will add a stalk to the flower so that it looks like the one below. It doesn't matter if you don't get it right first time – just type cs to clear the drawing screen, draw the flower again and have another go!

 When you have finished, write the LOGO commands you used in the space labelled Drawing a flower on Worksheet 5.1.

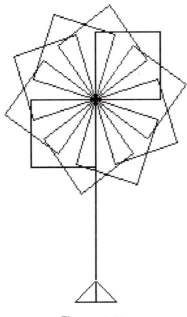

Figure 5.13

Next you are going to create a procedure that will draw a flower using the commands you have written on Worksheet 5.1. Follow the instructions below to do this.

 Click in the input box.

 Type edit "flower

Press **Enter** and the Editor dialogue box will appear.

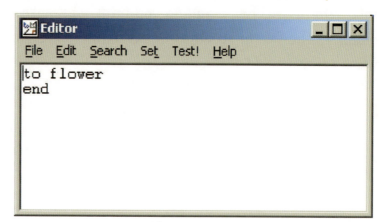

Figure 5.14

 Click after the word **flower** on the first line of the procedure.

 Press **Enter**.

 Enter the LOGO commands you have written in the box labelled **Drawing a flower** on **Worksheet 5.1**.

 Click **File**, **Save and Exit** on the Editor dialogue box menu.

Now try this procedure out and see if it works.

 Click in the input box.

 Type **flower**

 Press **Enter**.
LOGO will run the new procedure and draw the flower.

If the procedure doesn't work you will need to go back to the editor and check through the commands inside the procedure for mistakes. Follow the steps below if you need to do this.

 Click in the input box.

 Type **edit "flower** and press **Enter**.
The Editor dialogue box will appear with the flower procedure displayed inside it.

 Check through the commands and correct any mistakes.

 Click **File**, **Save and Exit** on the Editor dialogue box menu.

Now try using the procedure again – hopefully it will work this time!

Tip:

Edit the flower procedure and use different repeat commands to draw other flower shapes - one thing you might try is changing the angle of turn inside the repeat command.

Built-in procedures

LOGO has built-in procedures for drawing some shapes we will draw circles using two built-in procedures called circle and circle2.

Before we get started on this part of the chapter make sure your teacher has given you a copy of Worksheet 5.2.

 Load MSW Logo.

circle

This command draws a circle with the turtle at the centre.
To use this command you must tell LOGO what radius the circle must have.

 Click in the input box and clear the drawing screen.

 Enter the command circle 100

This command draws a circle that has a radius of 100 steps from the turtle at the centre of the circle to the edge of the circle.

radius
100 steps

Use the **circle** command to draw a picture like the one below.

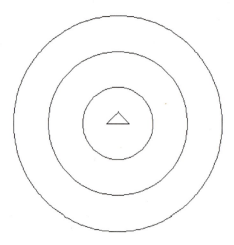

Figure 5.16

 Write the commands you used to draw this picture next to it on **Worksheet 5.2**.

circle2

This command draws a circle with the turtle on the edge. To use this command you must tell LOGO what radius the circle must have. The radius is the number of steps from the turtle on the edge of the circle to the centre.

 Click in the input box and clear the drawing screen.

 Enter the command **circle2 100**
This command draws a circle that has a radius of 100 steps from the turtle on the edge of the circle to the centre.

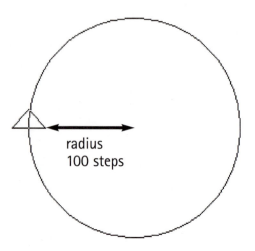

radius
100 steps

Figure 5.17

Use the circle2 command to draw a picture like the one below.

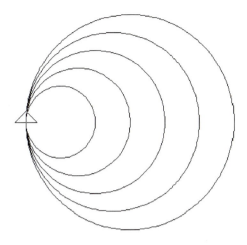

Figure 5.18

 Write the commands you used to draw this picture next to it on Worksheet 5.2.

Some other things to try

 Work out a repeat command that will draw the pattern shown below.

 Create a procedure called circpat1 that uses this repeat command to draw the pattern.

Tip:
You will need to use the **circle2** command and either the **right** or **left** command.

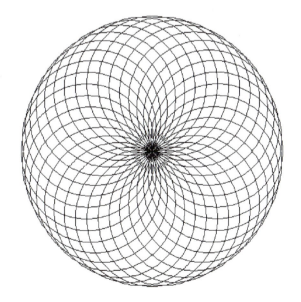

Figure 5.19

 Work out a repeat command that will draw the pattern shown below.

 Create a procedure called circpat2 that uses this repeat command to draw the pattern.

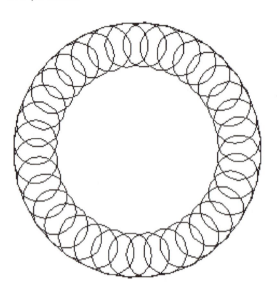

Figure 5.20

Tip:

You will need to use the **circle2** command, either the **right** or **left** command and the **forward** command.

Saving procedures

To save procedures you must use the save command. This command will save all of the procedures you have created using the edit command. There isn't a shorter version of this command so you will need to type in the whole word when you use it.

 Click in the input box.

 Type save "shapes.lgo
shapes is the name we are giving to the file the procedures will be stored in.

 Press Enter.
The file name will appear in the Commander window.

Note:

Your teacher might want you to use a different name for your file – ask first before you go ahead and save your procedures.

Figure 5.21

That's almost everything you need to know about creating procedures in LOGO. In the next chapter you will learn how to how to make procedures more useful by using variables.

 Close LOGO down.

Tip:

If you can't remember how to close LOGO down look back at the instructions on **page 12**.

Chapter 6
Procedures with variables

In the last chapter you learned how to teach LOGO new commands to draw shapes by creating procedures. In this chapter you will learn how to make procedures more useful by using variables.

Before we get started make sure your teacher has given you a copy of Worksheet 6.

 Load MSW Logo.

The next thing you need to do is load the procedures we created in the last chapter.

 From the main menu select File, Load...

Figure 6.1

 Click on the file called shapes and OK.
shapes is the name we gave to the file the procedures were stored in at the end of the last chapter.

Using variables in procedures

Suppose we need to change the square procedure so that it draws a different size square. We can do this by editing the repeat command inside the procedure and changing the number of steps in the forward command that draws the sides of the square.

 Click in the input box.

 Type edit "square

 Press Enter.
The Editor dialogue box will appear.

 Change the forward command inside the square brackets to fd 200

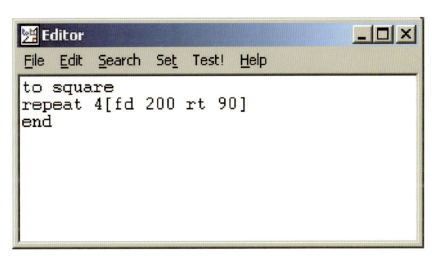

Figure 6.2

 Click File, Save and Exit on the Editor dialogue box menu.

 Click in the input box.

 Type square

 Press Enter.
LOGO will run the procedure and draw a bigger square.

The problem with this is every time we need a different size square the commands inside the square procedure must be changed.
A better method is to use a variable inside the procedure. Follow the steps below to add a variable to the square procedure.

Tip:
A variable is a value inside a procedure that can be changed whenever the procedure is used.

43

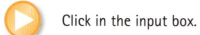 Click in the input box.

 Type edit "square

 Press Enter.
The Editor dialogue box will appear.

Change the commands inside the square procedure so that they are the same as those shown below.

```
to square :side
repeat 4 [fd :side rt 90]
end
```

Figure 6.3

Let's look at what the new commands inside this procedure mean.

The command :side in the first line of the procedure tells LOGO to expect a value for a variable called side to be given after the procedure's name.

The command fd :side inside the repeat command tells LOGO to use the value given for side as the number of steps to move forward.

Whenever this procedure is used from now on a value for side must also be given after its name. This value will be used inside the procedure to draw the square.

 Click File, Save and Exit on the Editor dialogue box menu.

Now we can draw different size squares with the square procedure by using different values for the variable side.

 Click in the input box and enter these commands:

square 100

square 200

square 300

Has the turtle drawn three squares like those shown below?

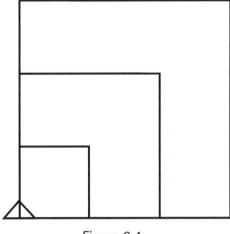

Figure 6.4

Next let's try adding a variable to the triangle procedure.

 Click in the input box.

 Type edit "triangle and press Enter.
The Editor dialogue box will appear.

 Change the commands inside the triangle procedure so that they are the same as those shown below.

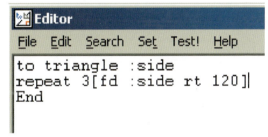

```
Editor
File  Edit  Search  Set  Test!  Help
to triangle :side
repeat 3[fd :side rt 120]
End
```

Figure 6.5

Now try using the triangle procedure with different values for the variable side – can you draw a picture like Figure 6.6?

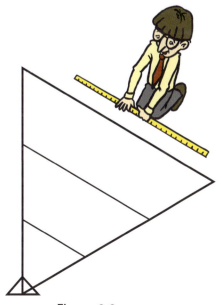

Figure 6.6

Tip:

If you're not sure how to do this look back to **page 44** to remind yourself how we used different variables with the **square** procedure.

Try this:

Use the **square** and **triangle** procedures together inside a repeat command and see what sort of patterns you can get the turtle to draw.

Tip:

Clear the drawing screen before entering each command.

Now try this

The square procedure can be used inside a repeat command to draw a pattern.

 Click in the input box and clear the drawing screen.

 Enter this command:

repeat 80[square 100 rt 5]

We can do the same thing with the triangle procedure.

 Click in the input box and clear the drawing screen.

 Enter this command:

repeat 40[triangle 200 rt 10]

Now experiment with some repeat commands of your own like these to draw some more patterns.

That's all you need to know for now about using variables in procedures. In the next chapter you will learn how to use colours in LOGO. You will learn how to change the background colour of the drawing screen, the colour of the turtle's pen and how to fill shapes with colour.

Now we need to save our new procedures and close LOGO down.

 Click in the input box.

 Type save "shapes2.lgo and press Enter.
shapes2 is the name we are giving to the file that the procedures will be stored in.

 Close LOGO down.

Note:

Your teacher might want you to use a different name for your file - ask first before you go ahead and save your procedures.

Chapter 7
Colours and patterns

In the last chapter you learned how to make procedures more useful by using **variables.** In this chapter you will learn about using colours in **LOGO.** You will learn how to change the background colour of the drawing screen, the colour of the turtle's pen and how to fill shapes with colour.

Getting started

 Load **MSW Logo.**

The next thing you need to do is load the procedures you saved at the end of the last chapter.

 Click in the input box.

 Type **load "shapes2**
shapes2 is the name we gave to the file when we saved the procedures at the end of the last chapter.

 Press **Enter.**

Now we can start learning about some of the LOGO commands that are used to draw with colour.

setscreencolour

This command tells LOGO what colour to fill the drawing screen with. The shorter version of this command is setsc – this is the one we'll use. To choose or change the background colour you must enter this command followed by the number of the colour you want LOGO to use.

 Click in the input box.

 Type setsc 6 and press Enter.
This sets the screen colour to yellow – 6 is the number LOGO uses for this colour. Is the drawing screen on your computer yellow now?

Let's turn the drawing screen colour back to white before we need to put our sunglasses on!

 Click in the input box.

 Type setsc 7 and press Enter.
This sets the screen colour to white – 7 is the number LOGO uses for this colour. Is the drawing screen on your computer back to normal now?

Tip:
Take care with this command. Always use it **before** the turtle starts drawing because it will wipe away anything already on the screen.

setpencolour

Tip:
The numbers for all the colours are shown on page 52.

This command tells the turtle what colour pen to use as it moves around. The shorter version of this command is setpc – this is the one we'll use. To choose a pen colour you must enter this command followed by the number of the colour you want the turtle to use.

 Click in the input box.

 Type setpc 4
This sets the pen colour to red – 4 is the number LOGO uses for this colour.

Now let's draw a shape and see if the turtle uses the new pen colour – we'll use the square procedure to do this.

 Type square 100

Has the turtle used a red pen to draw a square with red sides like the one shown below?

Figure 7.1

Some other things to try

 Draw a red triangle.

 Edit and use the flower procedure with the setpc command to draw three coloured flowers like those shown below.

Figure 7.2

setfloodcolour

The setfloodcolour command chooses the colour that LOGO will use to fill shapes. The shorter version of this command is setfc – this is the one we're going to use. To choose or change the flood colour you must enter this command followed by the number of the colour you want a shape to be filled with.

Tip:

Use the **triangle** procedure to do this.

Tip:

If you can't remember how to edit the **flower** procedure look back at the instructions on pages 35 and 36.

Click in the input box and clear the drawing screen.

 Enter the command setfc 4
This command will set the flood colour to red.
To fill a shape with this colour we need to use
the fill command.

fill

The fill command tells LOGO to fill a shape with the flood colour.
The turtle must be inside the shape before you use this command.

Let's try using this command to fill our square.

First we must make sure the turtle is inside the shape like the one
shown below.

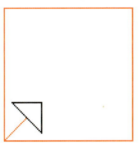

Figure 7.3

 Enter the commands below to move the turtle inside the square:

rt 45

fd 25

 Click in the input box end enter the command fill
This tells logo fill the shape with the flood colour.
Your square should look like the one shown below.

Figure 7.4

Tip:

Before you use
this command
make sure you
have used the
setfloodcolour
command to
choose the right
fill colour.

Question:

This shape would
look better
without the
turtle on the
screen. Can you
remember the
command that
hides the turtle?
Look back at
page 7 if you
can't.

Something else to try

Use the setpc, setfloodcolour and fill commands to draw three different coloured shapes like those shown below — yours don't have to be the same size or even the same colours.

Tip:

Use the **setpc** command to draw some coloured patterns.

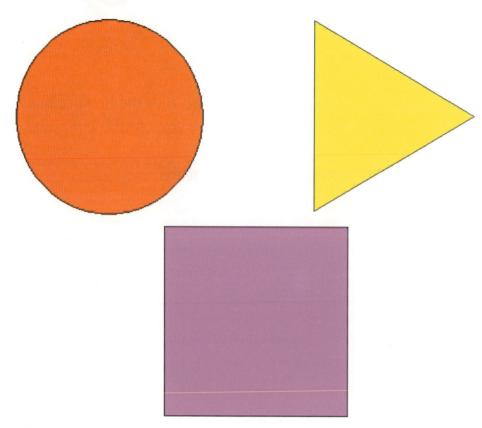

Figure 7.5

The LOGO colours you can use are:

0	black	9	brown
1	blue	10	dark green
2	green	11	turquoise
3	light blue	12	orange
4	red	13	lilac
5	purple	14	light orange
6	yellow	15	dark green
7	white		
8	dark red		

That's all we're going to learn about using colour for now. In the next chapter you will learn how to write a program in LOGO by building procedures to draw simple shapes and using them inside another procedure to draw a more complicated shape.

 Click in the input box and close LOGO down.

Chapter **8**
Procedures and programs

In this chapter you will learn how to write a program in LOGO by creating procedures to draw simple shapes and using them inside another procedure to draw a more complicated shape.

Before we get started make sure your teacher has given you a copy of Worksheet 8.

The shape you are going to write a program to draw is a house like the one shown below.

Note:

Worksheet 8 can be downloaded from the resources section at www.payne-gallway.co.uk/logo

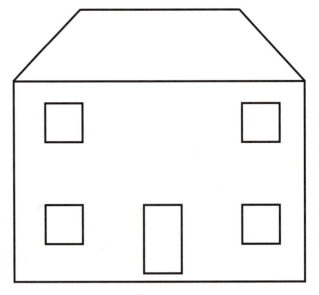

Figure 8.1

To draw the house you are going to create four procedures. Each procedure will draw a different part of the house. This will help to make the complicated task of drawing the house simpler by breaking it down into several smaller tasks. This is how computer programmers write computer programs.

Start by working out a set of LOGO commands that will draw the walls of the house so that they look something like the ones below.

Figure 8.2

 Write your list of commands in the box labelled walls on Worksheet 8.

Now you need to create a procedure to draw the walls of the house. You will use the commands you have written on Worksheet 8.

 Click in the input box.

 Type edit "walls

 Press Enter.
The Editor dialogue box will appear.

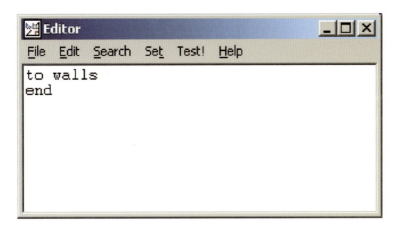

Figure 8.3

 Click after the word walls on the first line of the procedure.

Tip:

As you work through this chapter you will need to think carefully about the direction the turtle is facing before you draw each part of the house.

 Press Enter.

 Enter the list of LOGO commands you have written in the box labelled walls on Worksheet 8.

 Click File, Save and Exit on the Editor dialogue box menu.

Now follow the steps below to try this procedure out to and see if it works.

 Click in the input box.

 Type walls

 Press Enter.
LOGO will run the procedure and should draw the walls of the house. Follow the steps below to do this.

Next work out a set of LOGO commands that will draw the roof of the house so that it looks something like Figure 8.4.

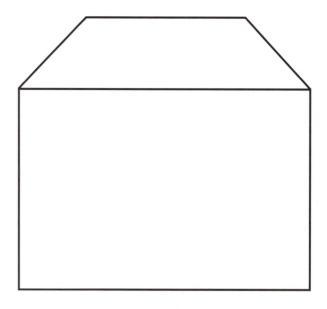

Figure 8.4

Write your list of commands in the box labelled roof on Worksheet 8.

Now create a procedure to draw the roof of the house that uses the commands you have written on Worksheet 8.

 Click in the input box.

 Type edit "roof

 Press Enter.
The Editor dialogue box will appear.

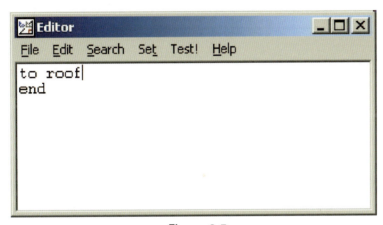

Figure 8.5

 Enter the list of LOGO commands you have written in the box labelled roof on Worksheet 8.

 Click File, Save and Exit on the Editor dialogue box menu.

 Click in the input box.

 Try this procedure out to see if it works.

Next work out a set of LOGO commands that will draw the windows of the house. They should look something like the ones in Figure 8.6.

Tip:

The windows are squares. You created a procedure to draw different sized squares using a variable in **Chapter 6** on **page 44**.

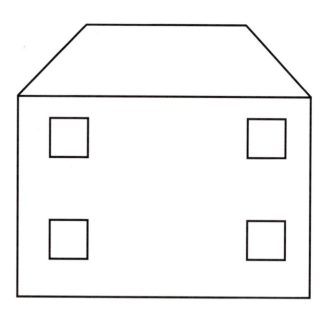

Figure 8.6

 Write your list of commands in the box labelled windows on Worksheet 8.

Now create a procedure to draw the windows of the house that uses the commands you have written on Worksheet 8.

 Click in the input box.

 Type edit "windows

 Press Enter.
The Editor dialogue box will appear.

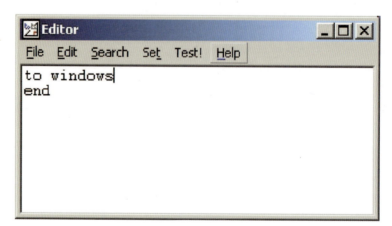

Figure 8.7

 Enter the list of LOGO commands you have written in the box labelled windows on Worksheet 8.

 Click File, Save and Exit on the Editor dialogue box menu.

Click in the input box.

 Try this procedure out to see if it works.

Now work out a set of LOGO commands that will draw a door on the house that looks something like the one shown below.

Figure 8.8

 Write your list of commands in the box labelled door on Worksheet 8.

Next you need to create a procedure to draw the door of the house that uses the commands you have written on Worksheet 8.

 Click in the input box.

 Type edit "door

 Press Enter.
The Editor dialogue box will appear.

> **Tip:**
> The door is a rectangle just like the walls. The commands you will need to draw the door will be similar to the ones you used to draw the walls.

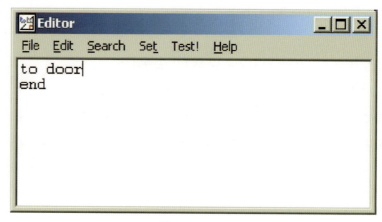

Figure 8.9

 Enter the list of LOGO commands you have written in the box labelled door on Worksheet 8.

 Click File, Save and Exit on the Editor dialogue box menu.

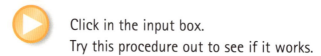 Click in the input box.
Try this procedure out to see if it works.

Finally we are going to create a procedure that uses all the procedures to draw the complete house.

 Click in the input box.

 Type edit "house

 Press Enter
The Editor dialogue box will appear.

Figure 8.10

▶ Enter the following commands:
walls
roof
windows
door

▶ Click **File**, **Save and Exit** on the Editor dialogue box menu.

▶ Click in the input box.
Try this procedure out to see if it works.

Now you need to save the procedures you have created to draw the house.

▶ Click in the input box.

▶ Type save "house.lgo
house is the name we are giving to the file the procedures will be stored in.

Tip:
If this procedure doesn't work click on **STEP** in the Commander window. This will run each command one by one and wait for you to click **OK** before carrying out the next command. Click on **UNSTEP** when you have finished.

Some other things to try

▶ Write a new procedure that uses the house procedure to draw two houses next to each other like those below.

Tip:
Move the turtle away from the first house and make sure it is facing in the right direction before drawing the second house.

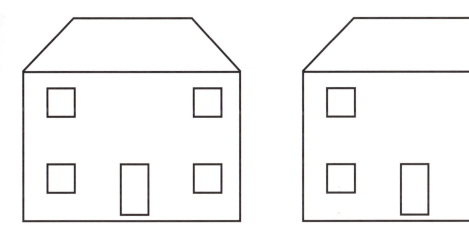

Figure 8.11

Use the **setfloodcolour** and **fill** commands you learned about in the last chapter to write a procedure that will draw a house like the one shown below.

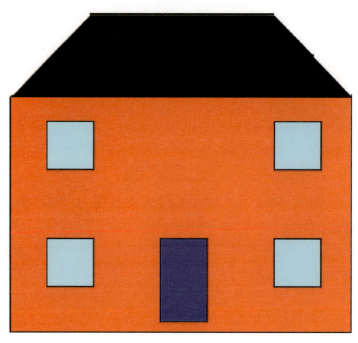

Figure 8.12

Tip:

Edit each of the procedures that draw the different parts of the house and add the commands needed for colour. Look back to **page 52** for a list of colours.

Write a set of procedures that will draw a rocket like the one shown below.

Tip:

Think about how many shapes make up the different parts of the rocket. Write a procedure to draw each shape.

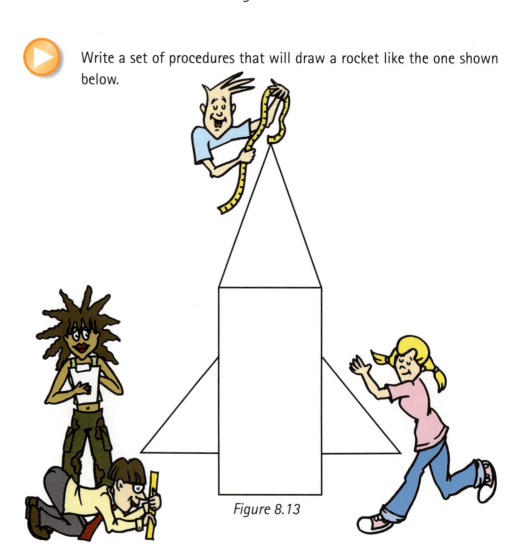

Figure 8.13

Write a set of procedures that will draw a train engine like the one shown below.

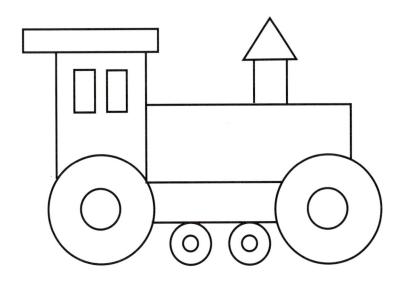

Figure 8.14

Tip:

Think about how many shapes make up the different parts of the train engine. Write a procedure to draw each shape.

That's everything we are going to learn about LOGO for now.

**It's the end of the book.
You have learned the basics of computer control using LOGO.
We hope you enjoyed it – well done!**

Index